Mrs. Twiggenbotham
Goes to a Party

To Jamie, Ryan & Leslie

May you always be filled with
the joy of the Lord.

Mrs. Twiggenbotham Goes to a Party

© 2003 by Emily King

Published by Kregel Kidzone, an imprint of Kregel Publications, P.O. Box 2607, Grand Rapids, MI 49501.

ISBN 0-8254-3065-8

Printed in Canada
03 04 05 06 / 4 3 2 1

Mrs. Twiggenbotham
Goes to a Party

Written by **Emily King**

Illustrated by **Rick Incrocci**

Outside Mrs. Twiggenbotham's cottage, an afternoon storm blustered through Smithville. As rain drummed against the windows, Felicity and her grandmother sat by a crackling fire. The old woman's knitting needles clicked away. Another rainbow-colored scarf grew—this one for Mr. Ringgold, the postman. In her arms, Felicity cradled Violet, her sixth Lovely Lassies doll.

Mrs. Twiggenbotham adjusted her glasses and studied her granddaugher. "My, my you're quiet. Felicity, dear, what is bothering you?"

Felicity slumped in her chair watching yellow and red flames lick the logs in the fireplace. "Oh, nothing, Grammy T.," she sighed.

"Come now, I know when something is wrong," her grandmother said. "That beautiful smile seems to be hiding somewhere today. Why, your face is drooping like those noodles in the chicken soup we had for lunch."

"Well . . . ," Felicity began, "there is a new doll in the Lovely Lassies Collection. Her name is Daphne. She's in the window of Talloola's Toy Shop . . . the doll with the golden curls and pink chiffon dress."

Felicity's eyes danced as she thought about Daphne. Then she sighed again and fiddled with the ribbons on Violet's braids. "But Mama and Papa say they can't afford her right now. I'll have to wait until my birthday."

"Well, my word," said Mrs. Twiggenbotham. "Honeybunch, what you need is a dash of God's joy. Of course, getting presents is fun. But God's greater joy is in giving."

Mrs. Twiggenbotham thought a minute. "I know!" she said. "You can help me make a delicious dessert for the Littles. Leonard Little has lost his job. Let's share some of God's love with his family today. Come to the kitchen, dear, and we'll see if we can find that smile."

Mrs. Twiggenbotham plunked a sack of flour on the table. "Let's make a Chocolate Cherry Delight. I'll pour, dear, and you stir."

Felicity turned the long wooden spoon, mixing dry and moist ingredients. She was a good stirrer, indeed.

"Do you think the Littles will enjoy our concoction, Grammy T.?" she asked.

Mrs. Twiggenbotham wiped her brow, leaving brown and white streaks above her flour-dusted spectacles. "Oh, I defin-UTE-ly, abso-TIV-ly think they will!"

"Then I defin-UTE-ly, abso-TIV-ly think so, too," chuckled Felicity.

Felicity and her grandmother set out to deliver an exquisite Chocolate Cherry Delight to the Littles. A surprise gust of wind splattered the entry hall with big, wet drops. Glistening orange and gold leaves whirled and swirled and flew in the door. Lily, the dear little kitty, pounced and batted them to the floor.

"My! What lovely autumn showers God has made today,"
Mrs. Twiggenbotham remarked. "Better get our slickers and
galoshes, Felicity. Then we're off to see the Littles."

Felicity loved walking in the rain with Grammy T. For even with her glasses perched perfectly on her nose, Grammy couldn't see the puddles very well. But she didn't mind the splashing at all.

"My word, there's another puddle," Mrs. Twiggenbotham chuckled. "Didn't disturb any ducks, now, did we?"

They splashed and giggled their way down Lemon Tree Lane to where it met Periwinkle Drive.

"Here we are at the Little's little cottage at the corner. Ring the bell, dear," the old woman said.

Felicity stood on tiptoes and pushed her thumb on the round white button.

The door flew open. There stood Leonard Little. "Why, it's Mrs. Twiggenbotham. And is this Felicity? I declare! How you've grown," he crooned. "But where are my manners. Please, do come in out of the rain."

"Look who has come to see us, Lottie," he said to his wife as she, too, came to answer the door.

"How nice of you to visit," Lottie said. "Please follow me to the warm front parlor, and let me take those dripping raincoats."

"Greetings, Mrs. Twiggenbotham," said Lattimer, the oldest child and tallest Little.

"Good afternoon," said Lambert, the middle Little.

Down the stair railing slid Leotta, the littlest Little. "Hello, Mrs. Twiggenbotham. Hello, Felicity. Did you come for my birthday party? I'm six today, you know."

Mrs. Little blushed. "It's really a simple birthday dinner. Just some chicken noodle soup—Leotta's favorite. Can you stay?"

Mrs. Twiggenbotham smiled at Felicity and winked. "Oh, chicken noodle soup is one of our favorites, too. Leotta, we'd love to help you celebrate your sixth birthday—a very special one, indeed. It just so happens we brought a Chocolate Cherry Delight," she said.

"Oh, Mother," Leotta squealed. "God sent dessert for my birthday party!"

"Yes, He certainly did," answered Mrs. Little. "By the looks of it, a scrumptious dessert! And we will put six birthday candles on top."

"Yelp!" The Littles' dog sprang from the chair before Mrs. Twiggenbotham sat entirely down.

"Oh, my word!" she declared. "What a pretty puppy."

"That's Lollipop," said Lambert. "Mother and Daddy got her for my birthday last month."

"Yes," Leonard added, "that was right before I lost my job. Lollipop is another mouth to feed, but we all love her dearly."

"Puppies are most darling pets," Mrs. Twiggenbotham said.
"Such sweet and playful characters, for God has made them so."
She bent over and scratched the little dog's ear. "From now on,
Lollipop, I'll be saving some tasty leftovers for you."

Mrs. Little set a plump tureen of steaming soup and a plate of crusty bread on the table. They sat at their places and held hands.

Leonard prayed, "Lord, thank you for this meal, for these friends, and for this special day—our sweet Leotta's sixth birthday! Amen."

They slurped every drop and ate every noodle of the soup. Then Lottie lit the candles on the Chocolate Cherry Delight.

"Happy Birthday . . . dear Leotta . . . happy birthday to you," they sang. Leotta drew in a big breath and blew.

"Yay!" Everyone cheered and clapped. Even Lollipop yipped and wagged her tail.

After dessert, Leotta's dad announced, "Time for your present." He pulled a package down from the hutch.

Leotta tore into the box. "Oooo!" she cried. "New shoes."

"To wear to school," said her mother. "Do you like the color?"

"Oh, yes," said Leotta. She turned them this way and that. Then she held them to her nose and sniffed the new leather. "They're beautiful. And they smell good, too! Thank you, Mother and Daddy. Thank you so much."

Felicity sat quietly, waiting to see what other presents Leotta would get. Perhaps a new baby doll or cradle . . . at least a new dress or some pretty things for her hair.

But there were no other packages. Leotta just sat smiling and smelling her shoes.

"Well, we must be going," said Mrs. Twiggenbotham. "Felicity's parents will come to get her soon. Thank you for inviting us to your birthday party, Leotta. We had a wonderful time, didn't we, Felicity?"

Felicity looked from Grammy T. to Leotta and back to Grammy. "But . . . but . . ." she stuttered.

"What is it, dear?" asked her grandmother.

Felicity looked down at Violet and answered, "But I haven't given Leotta my present yet."

She lifted Violet, kissed her rosy cheek, and held her out to Leotta. "Her name is Violet. She is a very good listener and she loves tea parties."

Leotta's mouth dropped open and her eyes grew as round as teacups. "Oh, Felicity! Oh my! She is the most beautiful doll in the whole world!"

She cradled Violet in her arms and rocked her. "I've been praying for a doll for my birthday."

Leotta threw her arms around Felicity and hugged her tight.

"Thank you, Felicity, thank you. I hope you will come back soon. We'll have a tea party—you and I and Violet."

"I'd like that very much," said Felicity.

"Felicity, giving your doll to Leotta was a generous and loving thing to do," said Mrs. Twiggenbotham.

"Well, Leotta's new shoes are very nice," Felicity answered. "And I'm sure Mr. and Mrs. Little would have given Leotta a doll if they could."

Felicity looked into Grammy T.'s eyes. It was true she couldn't see very far, even with glasses perched perfectly on her nose. But her grandmother's eyes sparkled with love and wisdom.

"You know, Grammy T.," she said, "you were right."

"About what, honeybunch?" she asked, tenderly smoothing the little girl's hair.

Felicity answered, "Getting presents is lots of fun. But God's greater joy is in giving. It even feels like my heart is smiling."

And do you know what? Felicity's face had found its beautiful smile, too.

Mrs. Twiggenbotham's Chicken Noodle Soup

Makes 4 brimming bowls

1 tablespoon butter
½ cup sliced carrots
1 rib of celery, sliced
1 green onion, sliced
2–14 oz. cans chicken broth
1 cup diced, cooked chicken breast
1 cup uncooked egg noodles
1 tablespoon dried parsley
¼ teaspoon salt

1. In a medium-sized saucepan, over medium heat, sauté sliced vegetables in butter for about five minutes.

2. Add remaining ingredients, cover, and bring to a boil.

3. Lower heat and simmer, covered, 10–15 minutes, or until vegetables are tender.

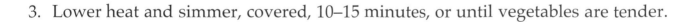

Mrs. Twiggenbotham's Chocolate Cherry Delight

(from scratch method)*

Makes 12 servings

Brownies:
¾ cup cocoa
½ teaspoon baking soda
⅔ cup butter, melted and divided
½ cup boiling water
2 cups sugar
2 eggs
1 ½ cups flour
¼ teaspoon salt
2 teaspoons vanilla extract
1 cup chocolate chips

Topping:
1 cup heavy whipping cream
¼ cup confectioner's sugar
1 ½ cup sour cream
1 teaspoon vanilla

1–30 oz. can cherry pie filling
slivered almonds

To make brownies:

1. Heat oven to 350 degrees. Spray a 9x13x2 inch pan with non-stick spray.
2. In medium bowl, combine cocoa and baking soda.
3. Blend in ⅓ cup melted butter.
4. Add boiling water. Stir until mixture thickens.
5. Stir in sugar, eggs, and remaining ⅓ cup melted butter. Stir until smooth.
6. Add flour and salt. Blend completely.
7. Stir in vanilla and chocolate chips.
8. Spread in prepared pan. Bake approximately 30 minutes. Cool completely in pan.

continued on next page

Note: All recipes should be prepared with adult supervision.